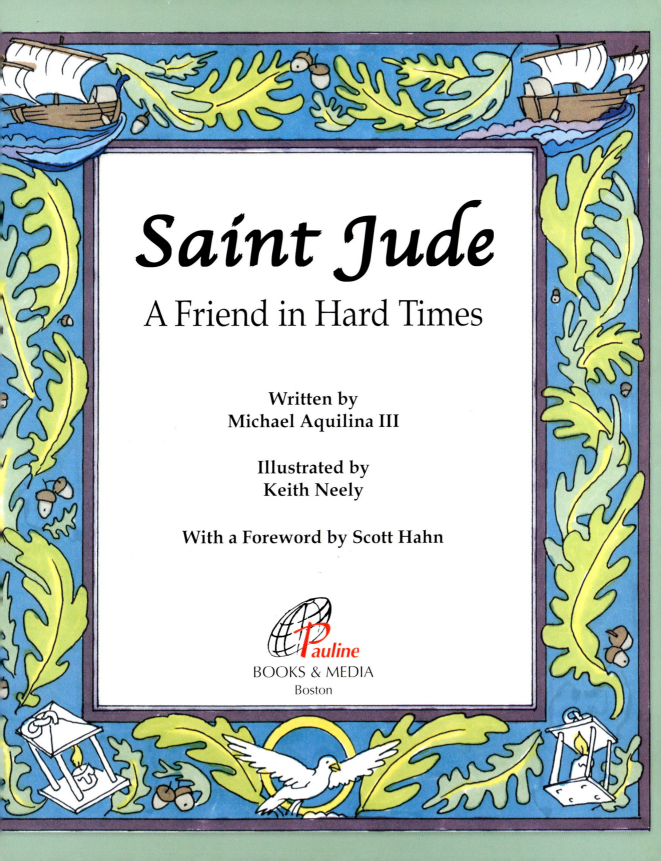

Saint Jude

A Friend in Hard Times

Written by
Michael Aquilina III

Illustrated by
Keith Neely

With a Foreword by Scott Hahn

Pauline
BOOKS & MEDIA
Boston

Library of Congress Cataloging in Publication Data is on file at the Library of Congress.

Printed in Korea and published in the U.S.A. by Pauline Books & Media, 50 Saint Pauls Avenue, Boston, MA 02130-3491.

www. pauline.org

Pauline Books & Media is the publishing house of the Daughters of St. Paul, an international congregation of women religious serving the Church with the communications media.

1 2 3 4 5 6 7   10 09 08 07 06 05 04

Contents

Foreword

The first time Michael Aquilina III visited my home, he must have been nine years old. He came to play with my sons, Jeremiah and Joseph, but he detoured through my book-lined office. He looked up at the rows of towering shelves and turned to me without hesitation, saying: *"You* should write a book about Saint Jude." It wasn't a request; it was a statement. And he repeated it on several other visits.

As a father of six, I've learned to be open to the Holy Spirit speaking through the mouths of children. I knew, however, that a book on Saint Jude was not in my near future, as I was already under contract to write several other books. So I told Michael: "I think God has placed that wish on your heart so that you might write the book."

That was the last I heard of the Saint Jude book—until, years later, when I received Michael's finished manuscript in my mailbox, along with a gracious invitation to write some words of introduction. I'm pleased to comply.

Since I became a Catholic in 1986, I've had a great fondness for Saint Jude. Early in my studies, I discovered that I was born on Jude's feast day, October 28, in 1957. For that reason—and

because I've always been a sort of "lost cause"—I believe this Apostle has watched over me with great care.

Like Michael Aquilina, I hope that many, many people will come to know Saint Jude's watchful care and his mighty prayer before the throne of God. The last book of the Bible, the Book of Revelation, shows us twice that Saint Jude holds a prominent place in heaven. God has blessed Jude as an Apostle, and so his name is on one of the twelve foundation stones of the heavenly Jerusalem (see Rev 21:18). As a martyr, too, Jude raises a powerful prayer, fully aware of what is happening in our lives on earth (see Rev 6:9–10). Even now, Saint Jude is very much with us, in that "great cloud of witnesses" (Heb 12:1), the communion of saints.

Michael Aquilina has written a book I could not have written, even though I am a teacher of theology. For every book of devotion is a special grace from God. My own books are God's gifts to me and my readers; this book is God's gift to Michael and his readers, among whom I am proud to be the first.

Read on, then, and walk the roads of life with Saint Jude. May the Apostle lead you without delay to share in the friendship and close family bond that he himself shared with Jesus.

Scott Hahn

ACKNOWLEDGMENTS

I'd like to thank Bishop Donald Wuerl, Dr. Scott Hahn, Fr. Ronald Lawler, O.F.M. Cap., and my parents, all of whom encouraged me as I wrote this book.

I'm also grateful to the ancient Christians who preserved the memory of Saint Jude in writing. Most helpful to me as I wrote this book were Eusebius's *Church History*, *The Teaching of Addai* by Labubna of Edessa, and *The History of the Armenians* by Moses of Chorene.

The quotations in Chapter 6 were adapted from *The Teaching of Addai*, translated by George Howard (Chico, California: Scholars Press, 1981).

Thanks to Saint Jude for favors received.

INTRODUCTION

Catholics have a tradition of turning to Saint Jude when they need help with a problem that seems hopeless —a lost cause, a desperate situation. We even call him the "patron saint of lost causes."

When their prayers are answered, many people follow the custom of publicizing Saint Jude's help. In the city where I live, there are many Catholics. If you look at any of the city papers on any given day and turn to the classified section, you'll find many ads that begin: "Thank you, Saint Jude, for favor received." Some even publish an entire prayer to Saint Jude along with their words of gratitude.

A few years ago, when I was seven, I discovered Saint Jude for myself. Someone had left a stack of photocopied Saint Jude prayers in the back of my parish church. They looked interesting, so I took one home. I was a computer fanatic then, and I had been having serious problems with my computer. In fact, my computer problems seemed hopeless…a lost cause…a desperate situation. This prayer seemed like just the thing.

I prayed the prayer, and in a few days I happened upon some software that would fix my problem—without any intervention from my local computer repairman. Immediately I realized that it was Saint Jude's doing.

Now, I'm older, and that computer problem seems small—hardly hopeless, far from lost. Now, when I read the paper and see how people thank Saint Jude, it makes the problem seem even smaller. They're thanking him for cures from awful diseases, jobs they found when they'd been unemployed for a long time, babies they had after years without children. Saint Jude came through again and again. Compared to these, my computer glitch doesn't seem to matter much. But it mattered to me then, and so it mattered to Saint Jude.

Devotion to Saint Jude is enormously popular. The most popular form is the novena prayer, which I include at the back of this book.

The words of the prayer are important, but they're not a

magic spell. I have to admit that I used to think of the Saint Jude prayer this way. If I only said it enough times, my three wishes would come true—just as if I rubbed a magic lamp.

Everybody who prays needs to learn that prayer isn't magic. Prayer is a conversation. It's a friendship between two people, and that means that the two people should get to know one another better over time.

In getting to know Saint Jude, we're making friends with someone who was a close friend of Jesus. It's not that Saint Jude answers prayers like God does. Saints are close friends of God who intercede for us, but it is actually God who answers prayers.

I think it's great that so many people pray the prayers to Saint Jude. But I wanted to go a step further. I wanted to get to know Saint Jude. I wanted to get to know him better.

That's not as easy as it sounds. Saint Jude lived on Earth almost two thousand years ago. He lived in a country that is much different from my own. He dressed differently, talked differently, ate differently, and even *slept* differently from me and my family and my friends. He didn't draw attention to himself, so we don't have many records of his life. There are no living witnesses I could call to prepare for this book.

14

So I've had to rely on the few ancient records that remain. Some of them are in the Bible. These are most reliable because they have been revealed by God. Some of Saint Jude's story has been preserved in the Church's tradition. In the Mass and in other liturgies, the Church has always remembered Saint Jude and praised him for his witness to Jesus. There is a third source for the details of Saint Jude's life, and that is the great accumulation of history and legend that has been passed down in the lands where Saint Jude preached. Some of this material is reliable and some of it may not be. Some of it, perhaps, was passed down by word of mouth for hundreds of years before someone finally wrote it down. Throughout this book, I will try to make it clear when I am relying on the Bible, on tradition, on history, or on legend.

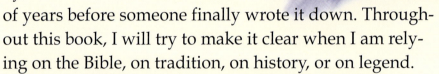

Even the Bible's account of Saint Jude is sketchy. The Gospels sometimes refer to Saint Jude among the Apostles, and other times as a close relative of Jesus. Some scholars believe that the Gospels are referring to not one man, but to two men who happened to share the same name. If I studied these problems for my entire life

and then two more lifetimes, I don't think I could solve them. So in this book, I'll be satisfied just to follow the traditions and legends that have come down in the Church.

What do we learn from all those sources? We learn that Saint Jude was one of Jesus' closest friends. In fact, he may have been Jesus' cousin. He was one of the twelve Apostles. He was one of the first Christian missionaries. He is named as the author of one of the books of the Bible. He traveled on foot to many lands to tell thousands and thousands of people about Jesus and to baptize them and help them start the Church in their lands. Even during Jude's earthly life, he worked many miracles with the power of Jesus. In the lands that we today know as Turkey, Syria, Armenia, and Iran, Saint Jude taught many new Christians to approach Jesus with great hope that they might be cured or delivered from sin.

In the end, Jude was willing to accept death rather than deny Jesus. He was brave enough to preach the Gospel to people who hated him.

I'm writing this book to share his story with many people today.

17

CHAPTER ONE
A Child of Judah

At the time Jesus was born, the land of Judea belonged to the Roman Empire. The name "Judea" comes from "Judah," the name of a man who had lived many centuries before Jesus. Judah was one of the twelve men whose families—and all their descendants—were considered the twelve tribes of Israel. All these tribes were related to one another, and the whole nation thought of itself as one family.

19

Of all the nations on the earth, this one family, the twelve tribes of Israel, had a special relationship with God. They were God's chosen people, and they lived in the country he had promised to them. Each of these tribes had its own lands, and the land of Judah was called Judea.

But, over the years, the tribes had many disagreements and disputes. They even went to war with one another. Some tribes were driven out of their lands by foreign invaders.

At the time of Jesus, only the tribe of Judah was living on its land. The tribe of Judah had an awesome history, including many famous ancestors. Perhaps the most important one was King David. Around a thousand years after King David died, the tribe of Judah numbered many thousands of people. During this time, two babies were born—descendants of Judah and of David. One was named Jesus (or Joshua). The other was named Judah (or Jude). History would come to know Judah as the apostle Jude.

In Judea, boys grew up learning the trade of their father. Girls grew up learning to manage a home, like their mothers. Nobody knows what kind of work Jude's father did, but surely the little boy was by his father's side during every workday. Some people think that Jude and his family might have been farmers, since farming was the most common work in Judea. In one ancient story about Jude, the author tells of how the Apostle plowed thirty furrows in the time it took a man to fetch him a drink. Perhaps plowing was a skill he learned from his father.

But there is more to life than work. Children learned from their parents how to pray to the God of Israel. They learned the law of God, and they learned about their nation's special relationship with him. They learned this

at home, from their parents. They learned it by attending a *synagogue,* or house of assembly, once or twice a week. And they learned it by making pilgrimages to the Temple in Jerusalem, the holy city, for the yearly holidays.

The children of Judea grew up knowing that they had a special place in God's plan. One of the children from

the tribe of Judah would be chosen by God to be the savior of Israel—and of all the nations and people of the earth. God had promised this to their ancestor, King David, and to his ancestor, Abraham. God had promised it again and again through the prophets.

In synagogue and at home, Jude learned about all these things. His parents knew that it was important to teach God's law to their children. When parents thought their child was ready to learn, they would begin the first lesson by placing a spoonful of honey in the child's mouth. Then they would teach the first points of

the law. That way, the child would always remember God's law as something sweet. As we'll see later on, Jude learned his lessons well. He always remembered the history of Israel. He always remembered stories of his ancestors. And he always kept in mind the importance of God's law.

Most importantly, he recognized the son of David who came to save the nations. That man was Jesus. During the time when Jude was growing up, many people were hoping that the twelve tribes would be reunited in one nation in the land of Israel, under one king. That king would be the promised Messiah.

During Jude's childhood, the people had good reason to believe this possible. Their king, Herod, had won back some of the lands that had belonged to other tribes. He had rebuilt the temple, the house of God, in Jerusalem. And many rabbis, wise teachers, were actively teaching God's law to the people.

Little Jude passed his childhood as many children did, in his day and in our day. He went to school. He made friends. He played games. He thought about what life would be like when he grew up. Maybe he made plans for those days. But God had a plan of his own.

CHAPTER TWO
Jude Gets His Calling

As Jude entered his teen years, he probably began to work full-time at his father's trade. Following the custom of that time, he and his father would work together, at least until it was time for the youth to marry.

Perhaps Jude was at work when he received his calling to be an Apostle. Jesus often called people while they were at work, inviting them to follow him. He called Peter and Andrew, James and John, away from their fishing boats. He called Matthew while he was working in his office as a tax collector.

If Jude was a farmer, then Jesus might have called him while he was plowing or seeding a field. Indeed, Jesus must have known some farmers and known them well, because he often told stories about farming. Once Jesus said: "Anyone who starts plowing and keeps looking back isn't worth a thing in God's kingdom" (Lk 9:62). In the fields of the Lord, Jude kept plowing and didn't look back.

Still, we don't know for sure whether Jude was a farmer, or when or where Jesus invited Jude to follow him. All we know is that he accepted Jesus' invitation and left behind his work so that he could travel with Jesus, learn from him, and become more like him. This must have involved great sacrifice for Jude, as the ancient books tell us that he was married and had children. In his land, it was common for men to marry as soon as they could work to support a family. Often, they married as early as sixteen years old.

Like the other Apostles, Jude honored Jesus as *rabbi*. When an adult began to study under a rabbi, he was seeking to gain wisdom to live a more perfect life and be more faithful to God's will and law. A student of a certain rabbi was called that rabbi's "disciple."

If Jude was expecting Jesus to restore the fortunes of Israel, then Jesus' teachings must have given him great hope. Jesus told the twelve Apostles: "Go only to the people of Israel because they are like a flock of lost sheep. As you go, announce that the kingdom of heaven will soon be here. Heal the sick. Raise the dead to life. Heal people who have leprosy. And force out demons" (Mt 10:6–8). Jesus even went so far as to promise his Apostles that they would sit on thrones to judge the twelve tribes of Israel. The Apostles, including Jude,

would take the place of the ancient patriarchs, the most important people in Israel's history!

Jude and the other Apostles had seen Jesus work many miracles. Now Jesus was giving them power to do the same. And they did. All the Apostles were amazed by the miracles they could work in Jesus' name. Word spread, and people gathered around the Apostles in great crowds, hoping to see a miracle happen or perhaps gain one for themselves. Some of the people were merely curious; others were desperate, clinging to their last hope. Certainly Saint Jude encountered both types of people.

The Apostles also met with people who hated them, people who were envious of the power God had given them. Some teachers resented the fact that these common workers—farmers and fishermen and a carpenter—were attracting more disciples than they ever could. Some people even wanted to kill Jesus and his Apostles. Jesus had prepared his friends for this, saying: "I am sending you like lambs into a pack of wolves" (Lk 10:3).

Soon, the Apostles had more work than they could handle. So Jesus appointed seventy-two more people to share the work and travel farther. An early Church tradition tells us that Jude worked among these seventy-two as well.

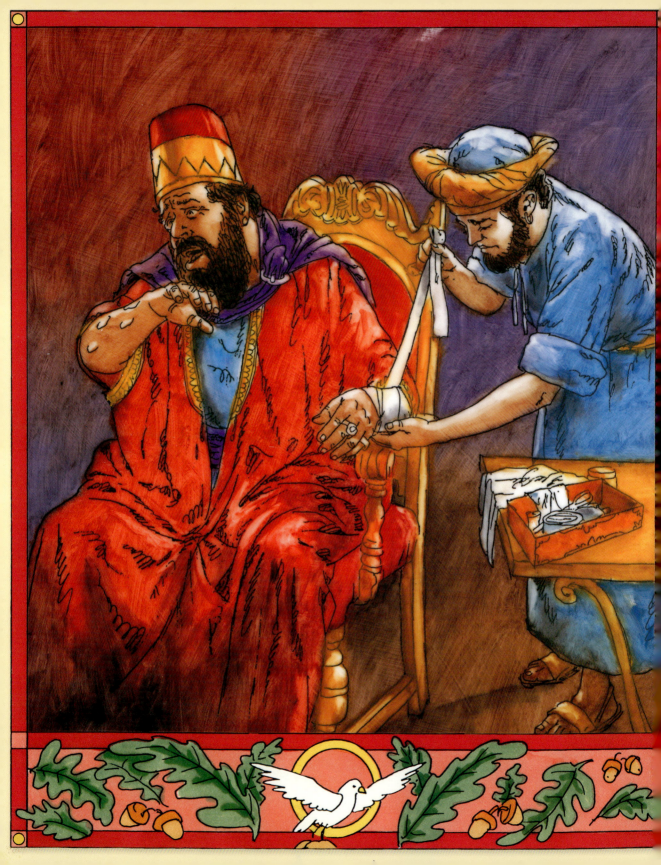

CHAPTER THREE
A King Sends for Jesus

Word spread of the wonders and miracles worked by Jesus and the Apostles. The stories passed from town to town, village to village, and soon through the country-side—even into nearby countries, like the far-eastern city of Edessa (in what is today Turkey).

In Edessa ruled a king named Abgar. He was a pow-erful and wealthy man. He commanded an army, lived in a palace, and had many servants. But in spite of all this, Abgar was suffering from the most dreaded disease in the world at that time. He had leprosy. Leprosy causes its victims' nerves to go dead. First, they can't feel parts of their bodies. Then, before long, they begin to lose por-tions of their skin. Leprosy leaves its victims disfigured.

31

In the ancient world, these poor people were expelled from their towns and made to live in caves near the gar-bage dumps. There, they picked whatever food they could from the piles of trash left by the people who lived in the town.

According to ancient histories, King Abgar was a younger man. He had been ruling the city since he was nine years old. Abgar was smart enough to recognize the early symptoms of the disease. He knew what was happening to him, so he called upon the best doctors of both his kingdom and the neighboring kingdom. They gave him potions and ointments, yet nothing worked.

The story continues that Abgar heard of a man, his same age, who lived far away in the kingdom of Herod —a man who was curing leprosy and even raising the dead to life. The man's name was Jesus.

Abgar wanted to go to Jerusalem to meet Jesus, but he could not because he was a king. If a king entered a foreign country, followed by his servants and guards, the country would think he was invading. So Abgar decided to send a message to Jesus and beg him to make the long journey from Jerusalem to Edessa to heal him.

It took a lot for Abgar, a king, to humble himself enough to beg from a mere carpenter who lived in a foreign land. But Abgar was desperate. He was clinging to Jesus as his last hope. Many people would say that King Abgar was a lost cause.

Abgar called for the royal historian, Hanan, and dictated a letter:

"This letter is from Abgar, King of Edessa, to Jesus, the good savior, who has appeared in the country of Jerusalem: Peace be with you. I have heard about you, and about the healing you have done without medicine and ointments. I have heard that you make the blind see and the lame walk. I have heard that you heal lepers and cast out unclean spirits and demons. I have heard that you heal those who are tortured with lingering diseases and you raise the dead. And when I heard all these things about you, I decided that you are one of two things: either you are God who has come down from heaven, or you are the Son of God. For this reason I have written to beg you to come here and heal the disease that I have. I have also heard that your own people complain about you and wish to do you harm. But I have a city, small and beautiful, where we could both live comfortably."

Hanan the historian wrote down every word. Then King Abgar sent him off to ride hundreds of miles on horseback to the land where Jesus lived. He traveled from village to village in search of the famous rabbi, and eventually he found his way to him. He approached Jesus, bowed down before him, and read him the letter from the king.

Jesus listened carefully and seemed to be moved by King Abgar's suffering and his faith. Jesus called to his

Apostle, Jude, and asked him to bring something to write with. According to a legend passed down in the eastern Churches, Jesus dictated the following reply to King Abgar: "Blessed is he who has never seen me and yet believes in me. Long ago it was written that those who see me will not believe in me, and that those who have not seen me will believe in me and be saved. But concerning your request for me to visit you: it is better for me to stay here and finish the work I was sent to do. After I have finished, then I will be taken up to him who sent me. Then I will send you one of my disciples to heal your disease and bring salvation to you and your people."

Jude handed the letter to Hanan. The messenger seemed disappointed that Jesus and his disciple were not returning to Edessa with him. But perhaps, in a sense, he could bring Jesus back to Abgar…. Hanan was a talented painter, and so he asked Jesus if he might paint his portrait for the king.

Hanan began to study Jesus' features. But the longer he looked, the more brightly shone a light from Jesus' face. Soon the light was so bright that he could no longer look at Jesus, never mind paint his portrait! Jesus felt very sorry for the man who had traveled so far at the command of a king. So he took a handkerchief and cov-

ered his own face. Then he handed the handkerchief to the painter. Impressed on the handkerchief was a perfect likeness of Jesus' face!

Hanan rode back home with his precious cargo. The trip seemed to go by in a flash. He could not stop thinking about the man he had met and the miracle he had witnessed.

Entering the gates of Edessa, Hanan rode directly to the palace.

He approached the king's throne and bowed down. Hanan expected Abgar to be angry that Jesus had not come. But the king was not. Instead, he asked many questions. He wanted to know more and more about Jesus—what he had said, how he had looked, the kind of clothing he had worn. The messenger told the king all he could remember, and still he couldn't tell the king enough.

Then Hanan handed Agbar the cloth with the miraculous image of Jesus. The king looked at it in silence for a long while.

For the first time in years, King Agbar seemed to be at peace. He seemed to have hope. One day, he would meet Jesus, or perhaps he would meet a disciple of Jesus.

CHAPTER FOUR

Jude's Faith Is Tested

Very few people showed the kind of faith in Jesus that we saw in the story of King Abgar. Indeed, many people hated Jesus and his Apostles. Jesus had warned the twelve that he was sending them out like lambs amid wolves. But perhaps they didn't take him seriously enough. Or maybe they just couldn't believe that anyone could oppose the teacher they loved so much.

41

They did meet opposition, however. Powerful people opposed Jesus and his mission—including some leaders of government and some religious leaders. Still, the Apostles stayed by Jesus' side.

Once, Jesus asked the Apostles if they planned to leave him because of the opposition they encountered. Speaking for all the twelve, Saint Peter said: "Lord, there is no one else that we can go to! Your words give eternal life. We have faith in you, and we are sure that you are God's Holy One" (Jn 6:68–69).

Like an older brother, Peter often spoke representing all twelve of the Apostles. But each of the Apostles also

spoke to Jesus one-on-one. On a particular night, after the Apostles had been with Jesus for a long time, they were all together celebrating the greatest holiday of the Jewish year. They were sharing the Passover meal. At that meal, Saint Jude spoke up, saying: "Lord, what do you mean by saying that you will show us what you are like, but you will not show the people of this world?" (cf. Jn 14:22). Jesus reassured him by replying: "If anyone loves me, they will obey me. Then my Father will love them, and we will come to them and live in them." (cf. Jn 14:23).

We can see by Jude's question that he cared for all kinds of people, not just himself and his friends. He wanted all the world to be as happy from knowing Jesus as he was—even those who seemed to be far away from Jesus. Jude stood up and spoke up for them. He showed himself to be a saint anyone can turn to, especially in times of desperate need.

The Apostles, however, were about to experience the greatest challenge to their faith. We have not mentioned the "other Jude" till now, but there was one, and he was also an Apostle. Most versions of the Bible translate his name as "Judas," to set him apart from Saint Jude. This "other Jude," Judas, betrayed Jesus. He knew that the authorities were envious of Jesus and wanted to see him

dead. So Judas helped them to arrest the rabbi on false charges—on the very night of that Passover meal that Jesus shared with his friends.

When the soldiers came to arrest Jesus, all the Apostles, including Saint Jude, were overcome by fear, and they ran away. They abandoned their friend.

Through that night and the next day, Jesus was questioned harshly by the soldiers and the government leaders. They tortured him; they beat him; they whipped him until his back was bloody and he was almost dead. Then they nailed his hands to a wooden beam and hung that beam on an upright beam, where they nailed his feet. There they left him, on a cross of wood, to bleed slowly and suffocate to death.

45

Where was Jude when all this happened? We don't know. Perhaps he was ashamed of himself and went to hide somewhere in the city. Maybe he found his friends, and they went together to mourn the loss of the greatest friend they had ever known—and repent the cowardice they showed when his life was threatened.

At the Last Supper Jude had asked Jesus why he was showing himself to the Apostles but not to the world. If only Jesus would show himself *now* to Jude and the others! Surely that is what they thought on that dark Friday afternoon.

CHAPTER FIVE

Jude's New Mission

Jude and his fellow Apostles took refuge behind locked doors in a small house in Jerusalem. They spent Saturday grieving. Some ventured out of doors, but even then they feared they would be recognized and brought before the authorities to receive the same sentence as Jesus.

The Apostles were sad. They were afraid. They were ashamed of themselves. Sunday, however, was a different sort of day. Some of the women of their group had set out before dawn to anoint the body of Jesus. But they found his tomb empty and ran back to tell the others the news.

Peter and John set out immediately to see for themselves. They, too, found the tomb empty. That night, Jesus gave them proof that he was risen from the dead.

Though they were gathered in a locked room, he appeared before them. He greeted them and showed them the wounds in his hands and his side. When the disciples saw the Lord, they were very happy.

Throughout the next forty days, Jesus remained with his Apostles, teaching them, working miracles, reassuring them, forgiving them, and preparing them to carry on his work when he returned to heaven. He told them: "I am sending you just as the Father has sent me." (cf. Jn 20:21).

The fortieth day after Jesus rose from the dead was a Thursday. That day he met his disciples at a mountaintop in Galilee. He gave them clear instructions: "Go to the people of all nations and make them my disciples. Baptize them in the name of the Father, the Son, and the Holy Spirit, and teach them to do everything I have told you" (cf. Mt 28:19–20). He also told the disciples to await the coming of the Holy Spirit, who would give them power—power to preach the Gospel in the whole world.

Then Jesus was taken up to a cloud and they could see him no more.

Ten days after Jesus ascended into heaven, fifty days after he rose from the dead, the Holy Spirit came down in the form of tongues of fire and a strong wind. After the Apostles received the Holy Spirit, they went forth with courage and a powerful ability to speak.

Now Jude had all he would need to set out on a missionary journey.

CHAPTER SIX
The Journey to the East

Far to the East, a man was waiting.

He was not sure what he was waiting for except the fulfillment of a promise. Every day, Abgar, the king of Edessa, awoke and went to the place where he kept his letter from Jesus and his image of the face of the Son of God.

51

Though Abgar appeared to be dying slowly of leprosy, he was really living in the hope that one of Jesus' disciples would soon come and cure him. He had heard rumors of Jesus' arrest and death sentence. According to an ancient tradition, Abgar had even tried to stop the execution by sending soldiers from Edessa. But they were turned back on the road by the soldiers of Rome.

Yet Abgar's hope still burned inside him. One day, as the story comes down to us, his messenger rushed in to say that there was a man in town—a powerful preacher from Judea, who was promising salvation…and speaking of Jesus! Abgar sent for the man at once.

Now, any time someone walked up to the throne of a king, he was supposed to bow or kneel before the king. But when Jude entered the court of King Abgar, it was Abgar who got up from his throne and dropped to his knees.

Abgar was trembling. "Are you the one Jesus spoke about when he sent me a message—that he would send one of his followers to cure me and to save my people?" he asked.

Jude replied: "Because you believed in him, Jesus has sent me to you."

"I believe in him!" the king said, "with such faith that, if the Roman army had not stopped me, I would have sent my own army to rescue him from crucifixion."

53

"Jesus fulfilled the will of the Father," said Saint Jude. "And death could not keep him. After three days in the tomb, he rose in glory and entered heaven triumphantly."

Then, approaching the king, Jude laid hands on him. Abgar felt himself instantly cured!

Next Abgar asked for Baptism, and he called the citizens of Edessa together to hear the word of God preached by Jude. The people responded enthusiasti-

cally, and King Abgar declared Christianity to be the official religion of Edessa.

Many people came to Jude asking to be healed of their illnesses, as King Abgar was. Jude did heal many of them, but he also made sure that they understood who he was, and who he wasn't. "I am not a doctor of medicine as humans understand it," he said. "I am a disciple of Jesus the Messiah, the Doctor of troubled souls, the Savior in regard to future life, the Son of God who came down from heaven, became a human being, gave himself, and was crucified for all people.... Do not lose this faith. For you have heard and seen things that bear witness…to the fact that he is the adorable son and glorious God."

Edessa was the first country on Earth to be an officially Christian land. Many people converted to Christianity, and the pagan temples were transformed into Christian churches, though the king forced no one to accept the new religion.

Jude remained in that city for a while, preparing some men for the priesthood and naming one man to be bishop. He taught these men a way of celebrating the Holy Eucharist that people in the Far East are still using today. It is called the Liturgy of Addai and Mari. Addai is the way they said Saint Jude's name in Edessa, and Mari

was a disciple of Saint Jude and one of the first Christian leaders in Edessa.

Abgar continued to be a great supporter of Jude and the new Christian priests of Edessa. He told him: "As for those who teach the gospel with you, I am ready to give them large gifts in order that they might have no other work in addition to the ministry. Everything that you need to pay for church buildings, I will give you. You alone shall enter freely into my royal palace."

From Edessa, Jude set out on far-ranging travels. Ancient histories tell us that he worked with the Apostle Bartholomew in Armenia. He traveled alone to places like Lebanon, Syria, Libya, and Persia, where he met up with the Apostle Simon and worked with him.

57

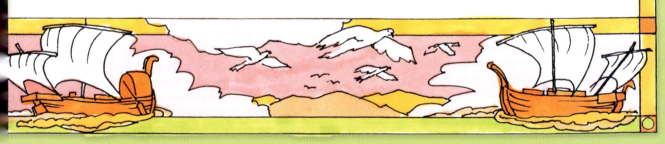

CHAPTER SEVEN
Jude Writes a Letter

Pick up a Bible. Start at the end and turn pages going backward until you get to the next-to-last book. That book is called "The Letter of Jude." Many scholars think that this letter was written by the Apostle Jude, who identifies himself here as the "brother of James."

The Letter of Jude appears on the earliest-known list of the books of the New Testament. That list, which is known as the Muratorian Fragment, suggests that the Letter of Jude carries the authority of an Apostle. Some modern scripture scholars argue that Jude *must* have written the letter, because why else would the Church attribute it to such a minor Apostle, rather than to "celebrities" like Peter, John, or James? Besides, why would the Church risk confusing people by listing an author whose name in Greek is the same as Judas's? These scholars conclude that the letter must have been written by Saint Jude, and that this Saint Jude must have been an Apostle of Jesus.

59

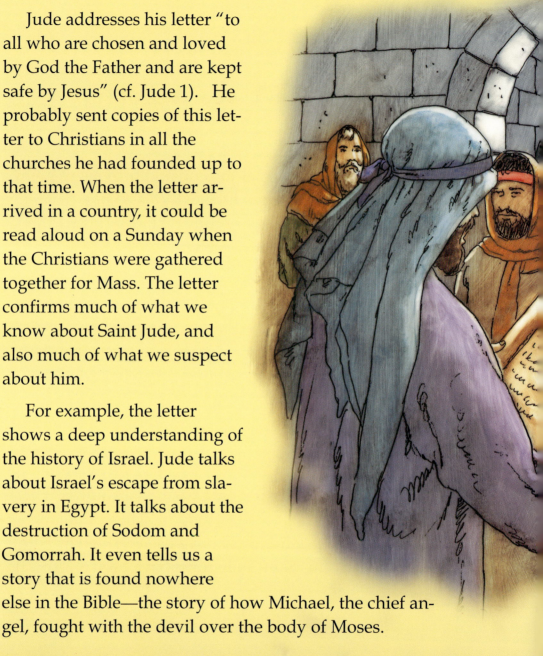

Jude addresses his letter "to all who are chosen and loved by God the Father and are kept safe by Jesus" (cf. Jude 1). He probably sent copies of this letter to Christians in all the churches he had founded up to that time. When the letter arrived in a country, it could be read aloud on a Sunday when the Christians were gathered together for Mass. The letter confirms much of what we know about Saint Jude, and also much of what we suspect about him.

60

For example, the letter shows a deep understanding of the history of Israel. Jude talks about Israel's escape from slavery in Egypt. It talks about the destruction of Sodom and Gomorrah. It even tells us a story that is found nowhere else in the Bible—the story of how Michael, the chief angel, fought with the devil over the body of Moses.

But Jude's chief concern in his letter is that some Christians in his churches were having serious misunderstandings about the Gospel. They were saying it was all right to break God's law because Jesus would forgive them anyway. "God is kind," they said, "and so it is all right to sin."

Jude had little patience for people who encouraged Christians to do evil things. He wrote: "These people are filthy-minded!" (Jude 12). And he urged Christians to remember the warning they had received from him and from the other Apostles, who preached that, "Near the end of time, selfish and godless people would start making fun of God. And now these people are already making you turn against each other… They do not have God's spirit" (Jude 18–19).

61

Surely we can recognize here the voice of the Apostle who had asked Jesus about showing himself to the whole world. If Jesus was going to show himself, Jude would make sure that people would see Jesus the right way, and not make up a fake "Jesus" who would be more to their liking.

CHAPTER EIGHT

The Last Days

Jude's work was more difficult in other places than it had been in Edessa. The people of Persia, for example, practiced a religion with a long tradition and strong protection from the government.

Jude and Simon met a lot of resistance in Persia. But they kept on teaching and healing people, winning some over to the faith and baptizing them. Some of the Persian religious leaders grew jealous. According to an ancient tradition, two in particular, named Zaroes and Arfaxat, denounced the Apostles publicly and tried to turn the people against them.

63

Zaroes and Arfaxat tried to counter the Apostle's miracles with magic tricks. But the Apostles kept exposing them as fakes and as men who were working with the devil. Eventually, word of this dispute reached the ears of the commander of the army of Persia. He came up with a test for the Apostles and for Zaroes and Arfaxat.

At the time, the Persian army was at war with an army from India. The commander asked Simon and Jude and Zaroes and Arfaxat to predict how the war would end. The Persian pair went first; they consulted the demons and told the commander the war would be long and bloody. The commander took this very hard. But the Apostles reassured him, saying that the army of India would begin to retreat the following day.

The next day's sunrise showed the Apostles to be correct. India's army came forward with terms for peace. The commander, furious with Zaroes and Arfaxat, ordered them to be put to death. They were spared only because the Apostles pleaded for them.

Still, Jude's opponents grew in fierceness, even as he moved on to new places and new peoples. One day, after he had traveled many miles through many years, Jude found himself facing an angry mob. Perhaps he remembered the mob that had come for Jesus on the night of his last supper. Perhaps he remembered how he and the other Apostles had run away in fear.

This time, he would not flee. The mob closed in on him with clubs and beat him until he was unconscious.

Finally, one coward came up and cut off Jude's head with a single blow of an ax. That day, Jude was once again united with his childhood friend, his rabbi and his savior, Jesus Christ.

CHAPTER NINE
Jude's Legacy

In the pages of the Gospels, Jude seems like a very quiet man. He spoke just one sentence. In the whole of the Bible, Jude wrote one letter, and it's the shortest book in the New Testament.

Yet Jude's legacy to the Church is huge. God wants us all to benefit from what Jude left behind and what he continues to bring to earth.

Jude is mentioned in all four Gospels, though he is sometimes called Thaddeus (a middle name) or Lebbaeus (a nickname) to distinguish him from the other Jude—Judas the traitor.

Jude left an example for his own children and grandchildren. In the years after Jude's death, they were rounded up by the emperor Domitian. Perhaps they were afraid, but they went forth bravely and spoke of their faith in Jesus. Domitian tried to take money from them, but he learned that they were not wealthy. So he lost interest in them.

Saint Jude is still revered in the far-eastern countries where he preached. In some of those countries, Christians have been punished for 2,000 years.

The image of Jesus that was sent to King Abgar was kept in Edessa for almost a thousand years. Later it was moved to Constantinople. Called the "Mandylion," or "little handkerchief," it has been copied many times and is revered by Christians around the world.

The Mass Jude helped to write, called the Liturgy of Addai and Mari, is still in use in the East.

Saint Jude's bones rest today with those of the Apostle Simon in a beautiful casket beneath the Altar of Saint Joseph in Saint Peter's Basilica in Rome, Italy. You have to search hard to find them. Only by peering over the altar rail can you see the names of the two Apostles.

There are two Saint Jude shrines in the United States. One is in Chicago and includes a relic of Saint Jude, a fragment of his bone. The other is in Baltimore. Both attract thousands of people every week of the year.

Besides being the patron saint of hopeless causes, Saint Jude is the patron saint of firefighters. We can be sure that when terrorists crashed airplanes into the World Trade Center towers and the Pentagon on September 11, 2001, Saint Jude was praying for the firefighters

who rushed to the crash scenes, imitating the courage and bravery of Saint Jude and all the Apostles.

Saint Jude is most revered today as the patron saint of lost causes. A rock group has even honored Saint Jude for his help in a song titled "Prayers to Saint Jude."

Why do we find Saint Jude so attractive when times are really hard? What is it that makes him the patron saint of seemingly hopeless causes? Maybe it's because—from King Abgar on—so much of Saint Jude's ministry was devoted to healing very sick people. Maybe it's because, at the Last Supper, Saint Jude spoke up for the outsiders, bringing them to Jesus' atten-

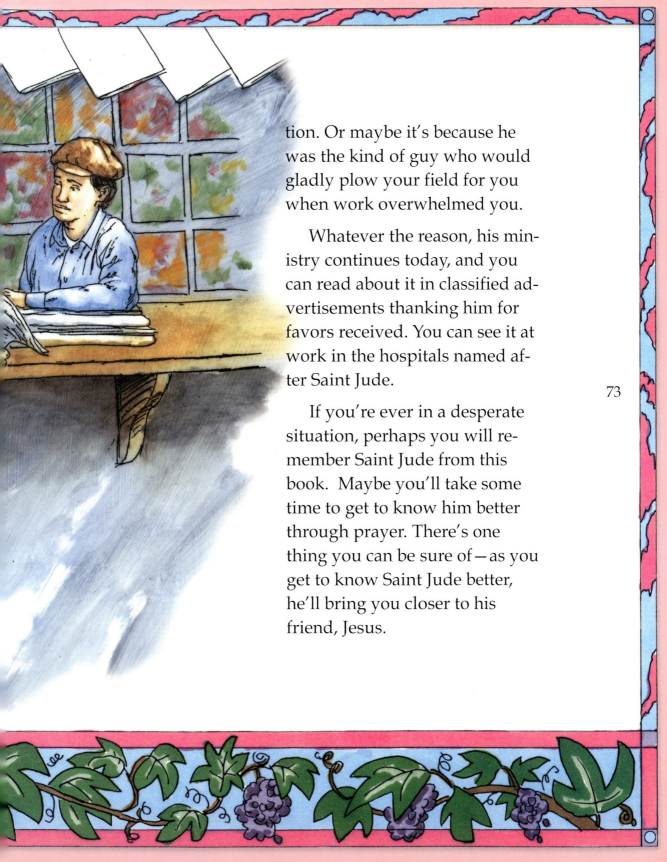

tion. Or maybe it's because he was the kind of guy who would gladly plow your field for you when work overwhelmed you.

Whatever the reason, his ministry continues today, and you can read about it in classified advertisements thanking him for favors received. You can see it at work in the hospitals named after Saint Jude.

73

If you're ever in a desperate situation, perhaps you will remember Saint Jude from this book. Maybe you'll take some time to get to know him better through prayer. There's one thing you can be sure of—as you get to know Saint Jude better, he'll bring you closer to his friend, Jesus.

Prayers to Saint Jude

Prayer for Help in Time of Need

(Most people say this prayer as a novena, which means that they say it once a day for nine days.)

Saint Jude, faithful disciple and friend of Jesus, many have forgotten you because of the name of the man who betrayed his Master. But the Church honors you, most holy apostle, and invokes you as the universal patron of hopeless cases—of things despaired of. I ask you to intercede for me now in my time of need. Please bring help where help is almost despaired of, that I may receive consolation from the Lord in my suffering and assistance in my distress, particularly *(make your request).* Trusting in the Lord's promise that whatever is asked in Jesus' name will be granted, I praise God for the many blessings I have already received from his generous love, and look to the day when I can glorify him with all the saints in heaven. Amen.

Litany in Honor of Saint Jude

(For private use)

Lord, have mercy.

Christ, have mercy.

Lord, have mercy.

Christ, hear us.

Christ, graciously hear us.

God the Father of heaven, *have mercy on us.*

God the Son, Redeemer of the world, *have mercy on us.*

God the Holy Spirit, *have mercy on us.*

Holy Trinity, one God, *have mercy on us.*

Saint Jude, relative of Jesus and Mary, *pray for us.*

Saint Jude, raised to the dignity of an apostle, *pray for us.*

Saint Jude, who suffered profound grief at the death of your beloved Master, *pray for us.*

Saint Jude, who had the consolation of seeing the risen Lord Jesus, *pray for us.*

Saint Jude, filled with the Holy Spirit on the day of Pentecost, *pray for us.*

Saint Jude, who led many people to faith in Jesus Christ, *pray for us.*

Saint Jude, who performed miracles through the power of the Holy Spirit, *pray for us.*

Saint Jude, who restored a non-believing ruler to health of body and soul, *pray for us.*

Saint Jude, who gloriously suffered martyrdom for the love of Jesus Christ, *pray for us.*

Blessed Apostle, with confidence we invoke you!

Saint Jude, helper of the hopeless, aid me in my distress!

Through your intercession, may the power of the Holy Spirit enflame generous members of the Church to proclaim the good news of salvation to all nations.

Lamb of God, you take away the sins of the world, spare us, O Lord.

Lamb of God, you take away the sins of the world, graciously hear us, O Lord.

Lamb of God, you take away the sins of the world, have mercy on us.

Pauline
BOOKS & MEDIA

The Daughters of St. Paul operate book and media centers at the following addresses. Visit, call or write the one nearest you today, or find us on the World Wide Web, www.pauline.org

CALIFORNIA
3908 Sepulveda Blvd, Culver City,
  CA 90230 310-397-8676
5945 Balboa Avenue, San Diego,
  CA 92111 858-565-9181
46 Geary Street, San Francisco,
  CA 94108 415-781-5180

FLORIDA
145 S.W. 107th Avenue, Miami,
  FL 33174 305-559-6715

HAWAII
1143 Bishop Street, Honolulu, HI 96813
  808-521-2731
Neighbor Islands call: 866-521-2731

ILLINOIS
172 North Michigan Avenue, Chicago,
  IL 60601 312-346-4228

LOUISIANA
4403 Veterans Memorial Blvd,
Metairie, LA 70006 504-887-7631

MASSACHUSETTS
885 Providence Hwy, Dedham,
  MA 02026 781-326-5385

MISSOURI
9804 Watson Road, St. Louis,
  MO 63126 314-965-3512

NEW JERSEY
561 U.S. Route 1, Wick Plaza, Edison,
  NJ 08817 732-572-1200

NEW YORK
150 East 52nd Street, New York,
  NY 10022 212-754-1110
78 Fort Place, Staten Island,
  NY 10301 718-447-5071

PENNSYLVANIA
9171-A Roosevelt Blvd,
  Philadelphia, PA 19114
  215-676-9494

SOUTH CAROLINA
243 King Street, Charleston,
  SC 29401 843-577-0175

TENNESSEE
4811 Poplar Avenue, Memphis,
  TN 38117 901-761-2987

TEXAS
114 Main Plaza, San Antonio,
  TX 78205 210-224-8101

VIRGINIA
1025 King Street, Alexandria,
  VA 22314 703-549-3806

CANADA
3022 Dufferin Street, Toronto, Ontario,
  Canada M6B 3T5
  416-781-9131
1155 Yonge Street, Toronto, Ontario,
  Canada M4T 1W2
  416-934-3440

¡También somos su fuente para libros, videos y música en español!